HISTORIC PLACES *of the* UNITED KINGDOM

PREHISTORIC SITES

John Malam

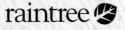

raintree

a Capstone company — publishers for children

Raintree is an imprint of Capstone Global Library Limited, a company incorporated in England and Wales having its registered office at 264 Banbury Road, Oxford, OX2 7DY – Registered company number: 6695582

www.raintree.co.uk

myorders@raintree.co.uk

Produced for Raintree by

White-Thomson Publishing Ltd
+44 (0)1273 477 216
www.wtpub.co.uk

Edited by Sonya Newland
Designed by Rocket Design (East Anglia) Ltd
Original illustrations © Capstone Global Library Ltd 2017
Illustrated by Ron Dixon
Production by Duncan Gilbert
Originated by Capstone Global Library Ltd
Printed and bound in China

ISBN 978 1 4747 5413 2
21 20 19 18 17
10 9 8 7 6 5 4 3 2 1

British Library Cataloguing in Publication Data
A full catalogue record for this book is available from the British Library.

Acknowledgements
We would like to thank the following for permission to reproduce photographs:
Adam Stanford © Aerial-Cam Ltd: 6, 12, 13, 15b, 16, 18, 20–21, 21, 32; Alamy: Heritage Image Partnership Ltd, 8, 26, 27 bottom, Robert Harding, 17, Skyscan Photolibrary, 9, 24; Copyright Cambridge Archaeological Unit: 22 left, 22 right, 23; Courtesy of the Portable Antiquities Scheme: 5 left (ID NMS-ECAA52), 5 middle (ID LVPL-9E5945), 5 right (ID WMID-A2FE55); Shutterstock: Andrew Roland, 19 bottom, Andy Usher, 15 top, Antonin Vinter, 4, Captblack76, cover, Claudine Van Massenhove, jps, 11, 14, Lizard, 31, Naluwan, 27 top, Pecold 28; Hans Splinter: 10.

We would like to thank Philip Parker for his help in the preparation of this book.

CONTENTS

Some words are shown in bold, **like this**. You can find out what they mean by looking in the glossary.

THE TIME BEFORE HISTORY

The first people arrived in Britain about 800,000 years ago. From then on, the time we call **prehistory** began. At first, people only had tools made from stone, but as time went on, they learned how to use metal. Prehistory in Britain ended with the arrival of the Romans in AD 43.

Standing stones like these are found in many parts of Britain. They were put up by prehistoric people thousands of years ago.

From stone to iron

People who study Britain's past divide it into different time periods. Prehistory is divided into three long periods known as ages. These ages are named after the most important technology of the time.

Stone Age

a period of about 800,000 years (about 800,000 BC to 2300 BC)

This **hand axe** is from Happisburgh, Norfolk. It was made by the first people in Britain about 800,000 years ago.

Bronze Age

a period of about 1,500 years (about 2300 BC to 800 BC)

This bronze axe head was made around 2000 BC. It was found in North Yorkshire and would have been used for chopping wood.

Iron Age

a period of about 850 years (about 800 BC to AD 43)

This iron knife was found in Staffordshire. It would have been used for cutting and chopping.

Dividing the Stone Age

The Stone Age is the longest period in prehistory. It has its own separate periods:

Palaeolithic or **Old Stone Age**: about 800,000 to 10,000 years ago.

Mesolithic or **Middle Stone Age**: about 10,000 years ago to 4000 BC.

Neolithic or **New Stone Age**: 4000 BC to 2300 BC.

How do we know about prehistory?

To find out what happened in prehistory, **archaeologists** search for clues about the past. They are "history hunters" who study the places where prehistoric people lived, worked and were buried. Archaeologists dig in these places, take photographs and make drawings. Then they write about what they have discovered. This is the only way to tell the story of what happened in prehistory.

Teams of archaeologists dig slowly and carefully to uncover the secrets of prehistory buried in the earth. This is a Stone Age settlement on Orkney in Scotland.

The first people in Britain

Sometimes, nature does the archaeologists' work for them and uncovers the past. This happened at Happisburgh in Norfolk, on the east coast of England. The sea washed away the beach to reveal a layer of ancient mud deep beneath the sand. Pressed into the mud were the footprints of adults and children. Archaeologists worked out that the footprints were made about 800,000 years ago by the first people in Britain. It was an important discovery.

DIG DEEPER

** JOINED TO EUROPE **

For much of prehistory, Britain was joined to Europe by a land bridge – a wide stretch of low-lying land. The first people in Britain probably came here by walking across it. As sea levels rose, the land bridge was flooded, and it disappeared under the sea. By 8,000 years ago, Britain was an island.

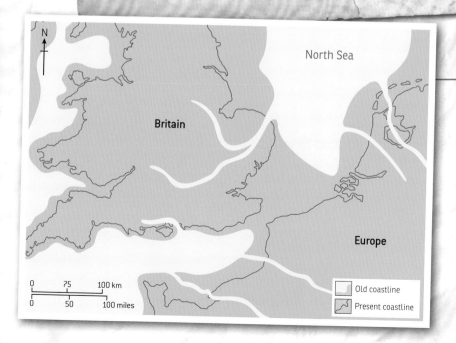

This map shows the land bridge from Britain to Europe, across which people and animals travelled.

North Sea

Britain

Europe

| 0 | 75 | 100 km |
| 0 | 50 | 100 miles |

☐ Old coastline
☒ Present coastline

GRIME'S GRAVES

There is a Stone Age place in Britain that's out of sight, deep under the ground. It's called Grime's Graves, but this site is not a graveyard – it's a mine. Prehistoric people dug deep into the ground searching for a type of stone called **flint**.

GRIME'S GRAVES

Brave miners

In many ways, Stone Age people were just like us. They were organised, worked together in groups and did different jobs. We see this at the Grime's Graves flint mine. The people who worked there were skilled miners. They knew how to dig through a soft stone called chalk using picks made from deer antlers. The miners used stones to hammer the picks into the ground. They then used the picks as levers to loosen the chalk and flint. It was dangerous work. Accidents must have happened, from slipping off a ladder to being hit by falling rocks.

WHAT: Stone Age (Neolithic) flint mine
WHERE: near Thetford, Norfolk
WHEN: about 2500 BC (4,500 years old)

wooden platform

wooden ladder

tunnels

This cross-section shows a flint mine at Grime's Graves. The largest mineshafts are 12 metres (39 feet) wide at the top and 13 metres (43 feet) deep. At the bottom, miners dug tunnels to get at the flint.

Best quality flint

Stone Age people dug more than 400 mineshafts at Grime's Graves in their search for flint. Flint was used to make everyday Stone Age tools. It is found in many places and can be picked up on the surface of the land. But the flint at Grime's Graves was the very best quality, so it was worth digging for.

Each of these hollows is the top of a filled-in Stone Age mineshaft.

Making a flint tool

Knapping is the word for shaping a rough piece of flint into a finished tool. Prehistoric flint-workers used **hammerstones** and antler hammers to quickly chip, or knap, the flint. As they struck the flint, small flakes were chipped away. Long, straight pieces called **blades** were also broken off. The flint-worker chipped tiny flakes off the blades to give them sharp edges for knives and scrapers. They also made arrowheads and awls (tools for making holes in leather and wood).

flint nodule

flint blade

This man is showing how a Stone Age flint-worker struck a flint nodule with a hammerstone. He has just chipped a blade off the nodule, which could be made into a knife or scraper.

Making an axe head

To make a flint axe head, the flint-worker chipped away at a piece of flint until he had the rough shape he wanted. Then he chipped smaller flakes from the cutting edge to make it sharp. It was then fixed to a wooden handle and was ready to be used.

cutting edge

On this **Neolithic** flint axe head, you can see where the flint-worker has chipped away small flakes to give the axe head its shape.

DIG DEEPER

** THE FLINT TRADE **

The black flint from Grime's Graves made excellent tools, which have been found all over Britain and Ireland. People travelled long distances in the Stone Age, taking their flint tools with them. Sometimes, the tools were traded from person to person.

SKARA BRAE

Incredible as it sounds, there's a village in Britain that was built long before the pyramids of ancient Egypt. This is the Stone Age village of Skara Brae, on the Orkney Islands. The houses that still stand there are more than 5,000 years old.

Homes under the sand

The Orkney Islands lie off the northern coast of Scotland. In 1850, a huge storm washed away part of a large sand dune. After the storm, stone walls could be seen poking out of the sand. **Archaeologists** cleared away the sand, uncovering the remains of ancient stone houses.

WHAT: Stone Age (Neolithic) village
WHERE: Orkney Islands
WHEN: about 3000 BC (5,000 years old)

These are the houses at Skara Brae and the passages between them.

Home sweet home

The village at Skara Brae is a group of about 10 small houses built close together. Their thick walls are made from stone. Narrow passages run between them. There are no roofs any more, but Stone Age people may have made them from turf or **thatch** laid on frames of wood or whale bone.

Stone furniture

The Orkney Islands are so windy that not many trees grow there. This means that Stone Age people would not have been able to make things out of wood. Instead, the Skara Brae villagers used local stone. They split the stone into slabs, which they used to make furniture.

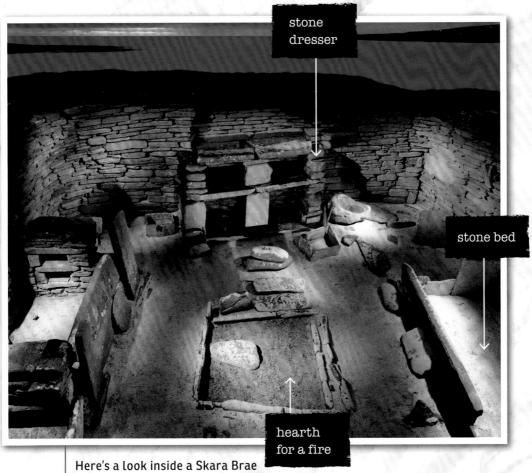

stone dresser

stone bed

hearth for a fire

Here's a look inside a Skara Brae house. The beds were probably filled with soft material, such as heather and straw.

Living at Skara Brae

Stone Age people lived at Skara Brae for about 600 years. Archaeologists think that only a few families were there at any one time. In the sandy soil around the village, they grew cereal crops, especially wheat and barley. They used the cereal grains to make flour for bread. The villagers kept cattle and sheep for meat and milk. They also caught wild animals to eat, including seabirds, wild boar and red deer.

Along the beach at Skara Brae, **limpets** were gathered at low tide and fishermen set out to sea.

Catching fish

Archaeologists found thousands of limpet shells outside the houses at Skara Brae. At first, they thought the people there may have eaten the limpets. However, the great number of shells suggested that the limpets were used for something else. Among the shells were fish bones. People may have used the limpets as bait for catching fish.

limpets clinging to rocks at low tide

DIG DEEPER

** ORKNEY'S SPECIAL STONE AGE PLACE **

At the same time as people were living at Skara Brae, Stone Age people were also busy a few kilometres away at the Ness of Brodgar. On this thin strip of land between two lochs, they built large stone buildings surrounded by stone walls. Archaeologists are now uncovering the buildings, revealing a mysterious prehistoric place. Nothing like it has been found in Britain before. Archaeologists think the buildings may have had a religious use.

There are more Stone Age buildings at the Ness of Brodgar than anywhere else in Britain.

BELAS KNAP

Just like us, prehistoric people cared for their dead. In the **Neolithic** period they built big tombs where many people were buried over a long period of time. Later, in the Bronze Age, they built smaller tombs that were usually for individual people.

Tombs for the dead

Belas Knap looks like a long, low hill on the edge of a field. This is a prehistoric place known as a long **barrow**, where Stone Age people buried their dead. There are four chambers, or rooms, inside Belas Knap. The dead were placed inside these chambers.

BELAS KNAP

WHAT: Stone Age (Neolithic) burial mound
WHERE: near Winchcombe, Gloucestershire
WHEN: about 3000 BC (5,000 years old)

Belas Knap is one of about 300 long barrows in Britain.

false entrance

earth mound

tomb entrance

Moving the bones

Stone Age people didn't leave bodies alone after burial. From time to time, they moved the bones around the chambers of a long barrow. Some experts think this may have been to make room for new bodies. Others think the bones were taken outside to allow the dead to spend some time among the living again. They were then returned to the tomb.

DIG DEEPER

** BRONZE AGE ROUND BARROWS **

A new type of burial **mound**, called a round barrow, came into use in the Bronze Age. Round barrows are mounds of solid earth piled up over dead people. There are about 40,000 round barrows in Britain. Some are on their own, but others are in groups, or cemeteries.

This is a Bronze Age barrow cemetery shown from the air.

STONEHENGE

There are many prehistoric stone circles across Britain and Europe. They are all different, but one similarity between them is that they are the work of many people. Stone Age communities worked together to plan the circles, find the stones and then move them into place.

STONEHENGE

Stones of Stonehenge

The stone circle Stonehenge is the most famous prehistoric place in Europe. The tallest and heaviest stones form the outer circle. They came from the Marlborough Downs, an area about 30 kilometres (19 miles) north of Stonehenge. Inside the main circle is a ring of smaller stones. These were brought 240 km (150 miles) to Stonehenge from the Preseli Hills in southern Wales.

WHAT: Bronze Age stone circle

WHERE: near Amesbury, Wiltshire

WHEN: between 3000 BC and 2200 BC (5,000–4,200 years old)

Stonehenge is the only stone circle with **lintel stones** on top of the standing stones.

3000 BC: ditch and bank of soil are dug

2200 BC: stones are placed in their final setting

lintel stones

Three stages of building

Stonehenge was built over a long period of time. What remains today is the last of three stages of building.

Stage 1 (about 3000 BC)

A wide circle of deep pits surrounded by a ditch and bank of soil is dug. This pit might have held wooden posts.

Stage 2 (about 2500 BC)

A circle of massive stones is placed. Smaller stones are arranged in a double horseshoe shape inside it.

Stage 3 (about 2200 BC)

The smaller stones are rearranged to make a circle. This is the Stonehenge we see today – a circle inside a circle.

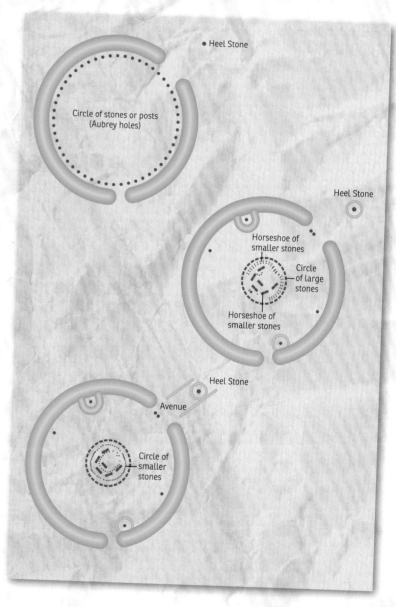

Heel Stone

Circle of stones or posts (Aubrey holes)

Heel Stone

Horseshoe of smaller stones

Circle of large stones

Horseshoe of smaller stones

Heel Stone

Avenue

Circle of smaller stones

Many **archaeologists** believe that the huge stones were moved using wooden rollers.

Here comes the sun

The people who built Stonehenge planned it carefully. The circle was designed to be precisely in line with the sun on two days a year. As the sun rises on Midsummer's Day (21 June – the longest day of the year), sunlight shines into the centre of the circle. After this, the days get shorter. On Midwinter's Day (21 December – the shortest day), the sun sets behind the tallest stone. From this point, the days get longer.

Why the sun?

Prehistoric people depended on the sun's light and heat to help them grow their crops. Experts think that Midwinter's Day was the most important day of the year. This marked the "turning of the year". The old year had passed and a new year had begun. It was time for farmers to get ready to sow their crops.

DIG DEEPER

** STONE CIRCLES **

Stone circles were built in Britain for about 1,800 years, from 3300 BC until about 1500 BC. Some are tiny circles only about 4 metres (13 feet) across, while the biggest are more than 100 m (330 ft) across. Many of them, like Stonehenge, kept track of time. They marked the movements of the sun or the moon, helping prehistoric people know when the seasons changed.

The Ring of Brodgar on Orkney is one of the largest stone circles in Britain and has some of the tallest stones.

On Midsummer's Day, the sun rises at Stonehenge at about 4:45 a.m.

MUST FARM

Must Farm is a group of about nine wooden houses built during the Bronze Age. The village was destroyed by fire about 3,000 years ago. What remains is like a time capsule that lets us see into the world of Bronze Age people.

Standing on water

Instead of standing on dry land, the houses at Must Farm were built above a river. The circular buildings, known as **roundhouses**, stood on long wooden poles called stilts. These stilts pushed deep into the clay at the bottom of the river. The houses were built close together and were surrounded by a large fence. The village was joined to the riverbank by a wooden walkway.

MUST FARM

WHAT: Bronze Age village

WHERE: near Peterborough, Cambridgeshire

WHEN: about 1000 BC (3,000 years old)

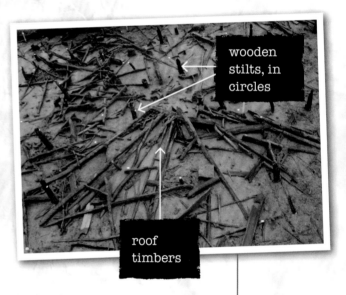

wooden stilts, in circles

roof timbers

the collapsed timbers of a roundhouse

Amber beads are just one of many finds that **archaeologists** have made at Must Farm.

The great fire

The fire destroyed the houses, but not everything was lost. As the stilts collapsed, objects fell into the river. There, they were buried in **silt** and **preserved**. Archaeologists found house timbers, cooking pots with food in them, bowls and plates, bronze tools, fabrics, glass beads and many other items. They provide a snapshot of prehistoric life there.

DIG DEEPER

** ANCIENT WOODEN WHEEL **

Among the objects found at Must Farm was a wooden cart wheel. This is the largest and best-preserved Bronze Age wheel found in Britain. It can tell experts a lot about travel and transport during prehistoric times.

An archaeologist excavates the wooden wheel. It is 1 m (3.3 ft) in diameter and is made from planks of wood joined together.

MAIDEN CASTLE

During the Iron Age, people built structures on the tops of hills. **Archaeologists** call these buildings **hill forts**. They were places where prehistoric people lived, worked and took shelter in times of trouble.

Power sign

The largest and most spectacular hill fort in Britain is Maiden Castle. Its ditches and **ramparts** twist their way around the sides of a hill, enclosing an area about the size of 50 football pitches. Maiden Castle was probably built by the Durotriges tribe, who lived in this area at the time. The hill fort could be seen from far away and was a sign of the tribe's strength and power.

MAIDEN CASTLE

WHAT: Iron Age hill fort
WHERE: near Dorchester, Dorset
WHEN: about 450 BC (2,450 years old)

Viewing Maiden Castle from the air reveals its amazing layout and structure.

Stop! Who goes there?

The builders of Maiden Castle put a lot of thought into making the entrance. After all, this was the way into the hill fort, and not everyone who came to the castle was friendly! As people approached the main gate, they had to walk along a twisting path. This forced them to walk slowly. All the time, people watched them from the ramparts to see who they were.

DIG DEEPER

** IRON AGE TRIBES **

Roman writers describe how, during the Iron Age, Britain was occupied by tribes. There were about 30 main tribes. Each tribe had its own territory and was ruled by a warrior king or chieftain.

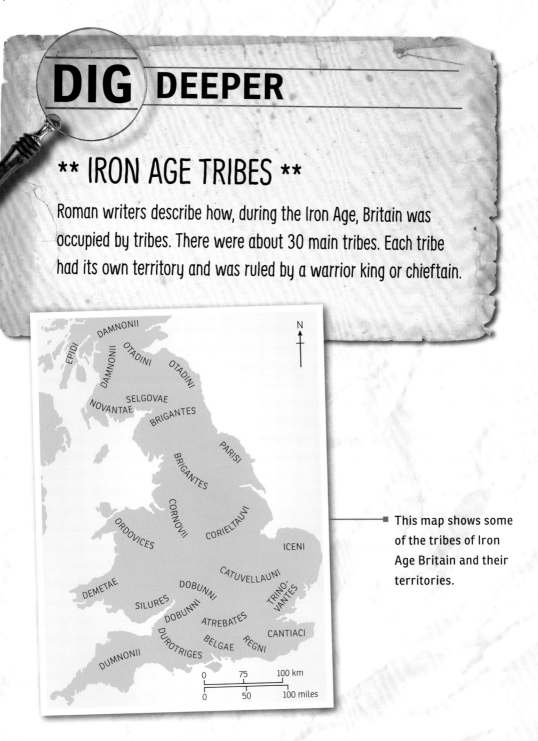

This map shows some of the tribes of Iron Age Britain and their territories.

Inside Maiden Castle

Packed inside the hill fort were wooden **roundhouses**. At its busiest, in the 200s BC, a few hundred people might have lived there. Archaeologists think that most people were farmers who worked in fields at the foot of the hill. At harvest time, wheat and barley were taken to Maiden Castle and put in grain stores. These wooden buildings were raised off the ground on posts to stop rats and mice from getting at the food.

This is how Maiden Castle's streets and roundhouses might have looked in the 200s BC.

DIG DEEPER

** BATTLE STONES **

Thousands of smooth pebbles were found at Maiden Castle. They were probably collected from a nearby beach. They would have been thrown at an enemy using a sling. These "sling stones" were found in piles, ready to be used.

Iron Age fighters used slings to fire stones from the ramparts of Maiden Castle.

End of the hill fort

In the 100s BC, a change came to Maiden Castle. Its ditches began to fill up with **silt**, and its ramparts were no longer well maintained. People abandoned the great fort that their ancestors had built. They moved away to live in villages in the countryside nearby. Hill forts in other parts of Britain were abandoned at about the same time. Iron Age society was changing.

LOOKING FOR PREHISTORIC PLACES

The story of Britain's **prehistory** is the longest tale ever told. It covers about 800,000 years, from the time the first people set foot in Britain to the coming of the Romans about 2,000 years ago. Evidence of prehistoric life and people is all around you – if you know where to look.

Signposts to the past

Some prehistoric sites are privately owned and are not open to the public. There are even some sites on Ministry of Defence land, where only military people can go. However, many of Britain's prehistoric places are looked after by national organisations. These are open for the public to visit and enjoy, and they are popular tourist attractions. Most of them are signposted with brown signs along the road to tell people where to find them.

These massive stones are all that remain of Legananny Neolithic tomb, near Banbridge, Northern Ireland. In prehistoric times, they would have been covered by a great mound of earth. There are many tombs like this scattered across the UK.

Organisations that look after Britain's past

There are several national and regional organisations that work to **preserve** and maintain Britain's prehistoric places:

England – Historic England

Scotland – Historic Scotland

Northern Ireland – Northern Ireland Environment Agency

Wales – Cadw (a Welsh word meaning "to protect")

England, Wales and **Northern Ireland** – National Trust

Timeline

800,000 to 10,000 years ago: PALAEOLITHIC OR OLD STONE AGE

This is also called the Ice Age because most of Britain was covered in thick ice. The first people in Britain arrive at the start of this period, about 800,000 years ago.

10,000 years ago to 4000 BC: MESOLITHIC OR MIDDLE STONE AGE

During this time, the ice melts and hunter-gatherer people move across Britain.

4000 BC to 2300 BC: NEOLITHIC OR NEW STONE AGE

During this time, people began to farm the land and live in villages for the first time.

3500 BC	The Belas Knap long barrow is built.
3300 BC	The first stone circles are made.
3000 BC	Skara Brae village is built.
3000 BC	Stone buildings are built at Ness of Brodgar. Their purpose is not known.
3000 BC	Work on Stonehenge begins.
2500 BC	Stones arrive at Stonehenge.
2500 BC	Flint mines at Grime's Graves are in use.

2300 BC to 800 BC: BRONZE AGE

Copper and then bronze metal come into use.

2200 BC	Some stones at Stonehenge are moved to new positions. This is the Stonehenge we see today.
1500 BC	The last stone circles are made.
1000 BC	Fire destroys a village at Must Farm.

800 BC to AD 43: IRON AGE

Iron, which is harder than bronze, comes into use.

450 BC	Construction begins on a hill fort at Maiden Castle.
100s BC	During this time, Maiden Castle and most other hill forts are abandoned.
AD 43	The Romans invade Britain, bringing the prehistoric period to an end.

Glossary

archaeologist person who learns about the past by digging up old buildings or objects and studying them

barrow mound of earth or stones placed over a grave in ancient times

blade long, thin piece of flint

flint type of stone that was chipped into shape to make tools

hammerstone heavy stone used as a hammer

hand axe chopping tool made from stone, usually flint

hill fort Iron Age place, usually at the top of a hill, where people lived, worked and could take shelter

knap chip away at a stone, usually flint, to shape it into a tool

limpet small sea creature with a cone-shaped shell, which attaches itself to rocks

lintel stone horizontal stone that rests across the top of two upright stones

Mesolithic Middle Stone Age period, 10,000 years ago to 4000 BC

mound small hill made of earth

Neolithic New Stone Age period, 4000 BC to 2300 BC

Palaeolithic Old Stone Age period, 800,000 to 10,000 years ago

prehistory period of time before written records

preserve protect something so that it stays in its original state

rampart wall or bank of earth surrounding a fort or castle to protect against attack

roundhouse round-shaped house used in the Bronze Age and the Iron Age

silt small particles of soil that settle at the bottom of a river, lake, or ocean

thatch covering for houses made from straw or grass

Find out more

BOOKS

Changes in Britain from the Stone Age to the Iron Age (Early British History), Claire Throp (Raintree, 2015)

Hill Forts (Prehistoric Adventures), John Malam (Wayland, 2016)

Mysteries of Stonehenge (Ancient Mysteries), Elizabeth Weitzman (Lerner Publications, 2017)

Skara Brae (Prehistoric Britain), Dawn Finch (Raintree, 2016)

Stone Age to Iron Age (Fact Cat: History: Early Britons), Izzi Howell (Wayland, 2015)

WEBSITES

www.bbc.co.uk/education/topics/z82hsbk
This site will take you back in time to find out what life was like in Britain during the Stone Age, Bronze Age and Iron Age.

www.bbc.co.uk/guides/zg8q2hv
An introduction to Stonehenge, describing what it was for and how it was built.

www.english-heritage.org.uk/visit/ places/maiden-castle/history/
A description of the great Iron Age hill fort Maiden Castle, with images of how it might have looked.

www.ks2history.com/skara-brae
Read a short description of the famous Neolithic village Skara Brae.

PLACES TO VISIT

Beaghmore stone circles
(a group of seven stone circles)
Cookstown, Northern Ireland, BT80 9PB

Bryn Celli Ddu
(a Neolithic burial mound)
near Llanddaniel Fab, Anglesey, Wales, LL61 6EQ

Callanish
(a magnificent stone circle on a Scottish island), Callanish, Isle of Lewis, HS2 9DY

Grime's Graves
(a Neolithic flint mine; visitors aged 10 and over can descend by ladder into an ancient mineshaft to see the flint)
near Thetford, Norfolk, IP26 5DE

Maiden Castle
(Britain's largest and most impressive hill fort), Winterborne Monkton, Dorchester, Dorset, DT2 9EY

Skara Brae
(the best-preserved Neolithic village in Britain), Sandwick, Orkney, KW16 3LR

Stonehenge
(the best-known stone circle in Britain)
near Amesbury, Wiltshire, SP4 7DE

West Kennett long barrow
(a spectacular Neolithic long barrow)
West Kennett, Marlborough, Wiltshire, SN8 1QH

Index